SCHOLASTIC

Let's Find Out
My REBUS Reader

I0890048

Kids Are Different!

by Karan Henry

SCHOLASTIC INC.
New York Toronto London Auckland Sydney New Delhi Hong Kong

Our 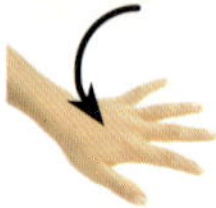 is different.

skin

Our  are different.

eyes

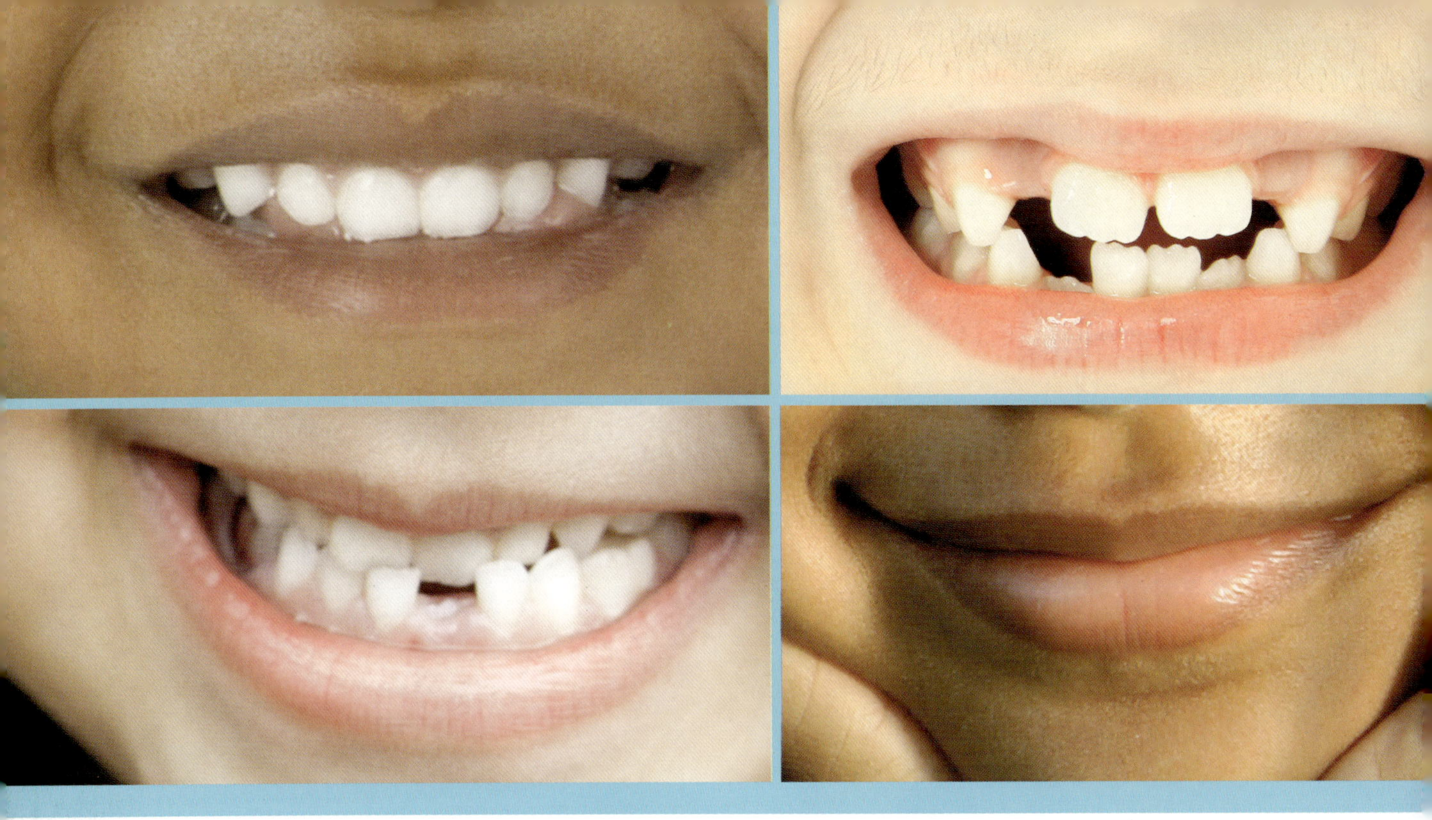

Our 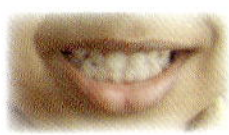 are different.

smiles

Our  is different.

hair

Our  are different.

clothes

Our  is different.

food

We are all  kids. That is the same!